Teenage Refugees From

VIETNAM

Speak Out

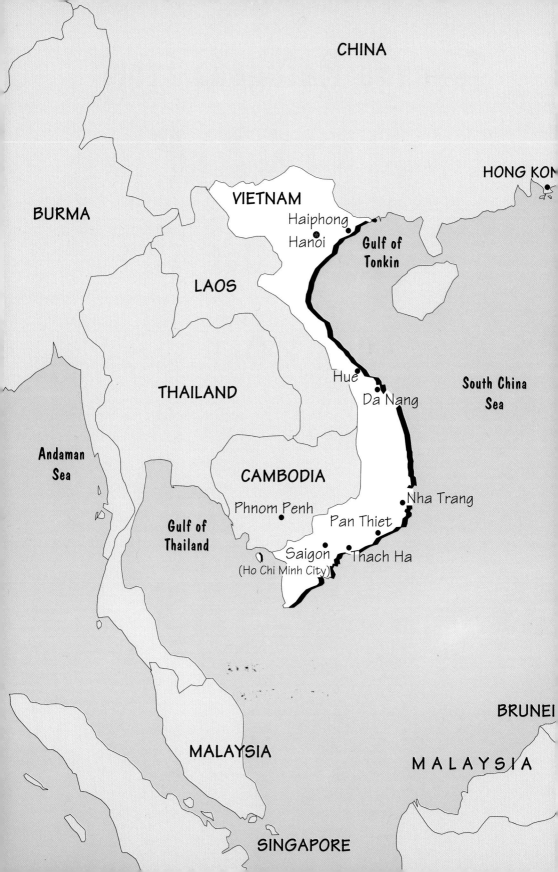

IN THEIR OWN VOICES

Teenage Refugees From

VIETNAM

Speak Out

KENNETH WAPNER

THE ROSEN PUBLISHING GROUP, INC.
NEW YORK

Published in 1995 by The Rosen Publishing Group, Inc.
29 East 21st Street, New York, New York 10010

First Edition
Copyright © 1995 by The Rosen Publishing Group, Inc.

Manufactured in the United States of America.

Library of Congress Cataloging-in-Publication Data

Teenage refugees from Vietnam speak out / [compiled by] Kenneth Wapner. —
1st ed.
    p.   cm. — (In their own voices)
Includes bibliographical references and index.
ISBN 0-8239-1842-4
1. Vietnamese American teenagers—Juvenile literature. 2. Refugees—United
States—Juvenile literature. [Vietnamese Americans. 2. Refugees. 3. Youths'
writings.] I. Wapner, Kenneth. II. Series.
E184.V53T44 1995
305.23'5'0899592073—dc20   94-40370
                                                               CIP
                                                                AC

Contents

Both outside influence and native culture can be found throughout Vietnam. Here are evidences of both: the brightly colored toys against the backdrop of ancient architecture.

INTRODUCTION

The people of Vietnam have been troubled by other peoples for many of the last 2,000 years. Vietnam has been invaded by foreign powers and has suffered civil wars. Yet through all this the Vietnamese people have endured, developing a culture that is a rich mix of their own heritage with that of the outside influences that have periodically conquered them. They have maintained a fierce spirit of independence.

Early Vietnamese civilization was influenced by close ties to the Indian region. The Champas, people with a Hindu-based culture, ruled Vietnam. Then the Chinese seized control in the second century BC.

China ruled Vietnam for more than 1,000 years, until 938 AD, when Chinese rule was finally overthrown by a Vietnamese warlord. After that, Vietnam enjoyed more than eight hundred years of independence. During this time the country was shaped by competing dynasties and warlords.

The religions of Vietnam include Buddhism (both Hinayana and Mahayana), Confucianism, Taoism, ancestor worship, Islam, and Caodaism. Caodaism is especially interesting; it is a home-grown Vietnamese faith based on a mixture of Eastern and Western thought whose practitioners communicate with the dead through a medium.

During World War II, the Japanese occupied Vietnam. Two million Vietnamese, a fifth of the population, starved during a terrible famine. After the Japanese surrendered in 1945, Vietnamese leader Ho Chi Minh, the man who was to figure so largely in Vietnam's future, came to power.

In the aftermath of the war, Vietnam was in chaos. Both the French and the Chinese were fighting for control of the country. Although he did not want the French to rule Vietnam, Ho negotiated an arrangement with the French to push out the Chinese. Ho explained why: "The last time the Chinese came, they stayed for a thousand years. The French are foreigners. They are weak. Colonialism is dying. The white man is finished in Asia. As for me, I prefer to sniff French manure for five years than to eat Chinese manure for the rest of my life."

Although France officially ruled Vietnam, chaos continued to reign. To reestablish control, the French shelled Haiphong in 1946, killing hundreds of civilians. The Vietnamese rebelled. The war between France and Vietnam had begun and would last until 1954. During this time, Ho and his troops based themselves in the dense jungles and rugged mountains of north central Vietnam. They began to perfect fighting techniques that would be used so effectively against the United States several years later in the Vietnam War.

The dire results of wars in and occupation of Vietnam by several different countries caused many people to try to escape by boat to neighboring countries, including Hong Kong. In 1990, there were more than 40,000 Vietnamese boat people in Hong Kong.

The United States armed forces were completely unprepared to deal with Vietnamese guerrilla fighting tactics.

The French withdrew from Vietnam in the summer of 1954 as part of an agreement drawn up at the Geneva Conference. It divided Vietnam into two zones, Communist north and anti-Communist south.

By the time the French withdrew, the U.S. had contributed over two billion dollars to France's war effort. Ho and his troops, the Viet Cong, were supported by the former Soviet Union and the new leaders in the People's Republic of China.

The U.S. threw its support behind the anti-Communist government of the South, led by Ngo

Dinh Diem. The U.S. sent in "military advisers" to help Diem maintain power. Diem's government was known for its corruption. In the early 1960s, people in the South rose up against him. The United States betrayed him in 1963, supporting a military coup that overthrew Diem's government and killed him.

In 1963, 16,300 U.S. military personnel were stationed in Vietnam. By December 1965, 184,300 U.S. soldiers were trying to overthrow Ho's Communist government in North Vietnam. In 1967, the U.S. fighting force had risen to 485,600; in 1969, to 543,400. Vietnam was ravaged by the war. The U.S. used napalm, a fire-causing chemical sprayed from the air, to destroy whole villages.

Ho knew that the Vietnamese will for independence would prevail. And it did. An active peace movement in the U.S. and continued resistance by the Viet Cong combined to force U.S. withdrawal from Vietnam. In January 1973, the U.S. signed the Paris Agreements, which called for a cease-fire between the U.S., South Vietnam, the Viet Cong, and North Vietnam—and a complete withdrawal of U.S. troops.

In 1975, South Vietnam fell to North Vietnam, and the last U.S. personnel were flown out of the embassy in Saigon. During the collapse of the South, 135,000 Vietnamese fled the country by sea, and in the next five years 545,000 followed, becoming known as the "boat people."

More Vietnamese fled the country in the 1980s,

Chử vắng nhà
Gà vọc niêu tôm

English translation from Vietnamese:
When the master's away, the chickens
will play in the shrimp pot.

when the Orderly Departure program was begun. It allowed Vietnamese to apply for visas to go abroad as political refugees.

Today, the economic policies in Vietnam have been eased and the trade embargo by the U.S. and its allies has been lifted. It is reported that many Vietnamese in the U.S. are returning to Vietnam and starting businesses.

* * *

Some of the teenagers interviewed for this book asked that their photographs not be used. Others wanted the world to know who they are. In all cases, we have used only the students' first names in order to protect their privacy.◆

This sixteen-year-old boy shines the shoes of a customer belonging to the new merchant class. The members of this new group are throwing away their customary plastic sandals in favor of leather shoes.

Binh, 19, came to the United States when she was eight years old from the fishing village of Pan Thiet in what was South Vietnam. Her father was a shopkeeper. After reaching the United States, Binh and her family settled in Farmington, Illinois. She is now a college student at the University of Illinois in Chicago. She is studying to be a pharmacist.

BINH
BRIBES OF GOLD

I was eight years old when I left Vietnam and came to the United States. I am now 19, a student at the University of Illinois at Chicago. When we lived in Vietnam, my mother delivered babies and my father owned a bicycle shop. We lived in the village of Pan Thiet (pronounced fang tea) in the south. It was on the sea, and most people were fishermen.

The main reason we left Vietnam was that the Communists took away my father's shop. Their motto was to take away from the rich and give to the poor. I guess we were considered well off. The police came with guns and shut us down. Then they sent my father to a reform camp in the jungles of the central highlands.

I remember there was a lot of controversy in my family before he left. My mom wanted to hide him. But the police kept looking for him and

As the free-market economy grows, state subsidies for health and education decrease.
Many people have been left hungry and looking for a means to sustain themselves.

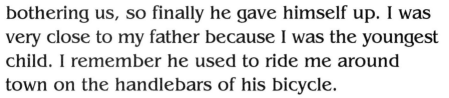
bothering us, so finally he gave himself up. I was
very close to my father because I was the youngest
child. I remember he used to ride me around
town on the handlebars of his bicycle.

My mother made trips to visit my father in the
reform camp. She took him food and clothing. It
was very dangerous. She had to walk through the
jungle territories where no one went. My father
came home when I was six. Reform camp had
worn him out. He died in our house.

For a long time my mother had wanted us to
leave Vietnam. After my father died, she sent my
older brother and sister abroad. They left by boat
in the middle of the night. When our turn came,
that's how we left. It was really scary. If we had
been caught we would have been in real trouble.
The police would have sent us to prison for trying
to leave the country.

The night we left it was very dark. We sneaked
from the house down to the river. My mother
bribed a guard with gold. The night was chilly. We
had to hide in the hold of a fishing boat, covered
with tarps. The boat stank of fish. We had to lie
there quietly in the stench as the boat rode down
the river, through checkpoints and out to sea. There
were more guards along the way. The boat owners
bribed them with cigarettes, food, and liquor.

We sailed into the South China Sea, and soon
we ran out of food and water. We were hoping to
be picked up by a ship from France, Great Britain,

or the United States. But first a ship from Taiwan picked us up. We begged for food and they fed us. They gave us one day's water and sent us back to our boat. We sailed some more, and, finally, after three days, an American ship picked us up. I remember the ship. It was huge. All these men in white uniforms looked down on us. They took us on board and gave us food. We took showers and slept. The next day they took us to Singapore.

It was weird stepping on land. I had been seasick the whole time and was very weak. For several months, we lived in a house with other refugees. Each family had a corner of a room. We had a gas stove, the kind you use when camping. We ate rice and noodles.

Fortunately, my older brother and sister were already in the United States. This helped speed up the paperwork for us. We flew from Singapore to San Francisco. We spent a couple of nights quarantined, being checked for illness and disease. Then we flew to Peoria, Illinois, and our family was reunited. There was a lot of crying. I was happy but confused, just a little kid, and it was really weird to see my sister and my brother looking so grown-up. They didn't look like Americans—not yet.

It was hard to adjust to living in a new country. We lived in cramped quarters. There was the language barrier. We were the only Vietnamese family in Farmington (Illinois). My mom had an especially hard time. My brother and sister were

Travel conditions were brutal for boat people, with cramped quarters and little or no food or water.

more independent than they would have been in Vietnam. They came and went as they pleased. They said whatever they wanted. It was the United States! When I go to see Vietnamese families I feel awkward with the rigid formalities, like how you're supposed to greet people. Or that you can't pick up a tea glass before an adult does. Or that kids are not supposed to speak unless they are spoken to first.

At first, I didn't feel entirely comfortable in my new life. American kids surrounded us. They talked to us, and we didn't know what they were saying. But I picked up English fast because I was young. I entered public school in the second grade. People made fun of us because our skin was

Foreign business interests are evident throughout Vietnam.

different. They called us chocolate, and I wanted to punch them.

I don't know much about the Vietnam War because I was so young. I remember there was bombing at our house, and Mom took us to the beachhouse and hid me under the bed. I think about going back to Vietnam and seeing my step-brothers and sisters. I write to them occasionally. One works for the government. A month ago we made our first phone call to Vietnam. My step-sister got on the speaker phone. My mom said her voice sounded older and different.

I love going to school in Chicago. I want to study to be a pharmacist. It's neat to meet people from so many different cultures. Everyone who first appears to be American isn't really American. They are Romanian or Italian or Russian. The cultural diversity is amazing and totally interesting, and I love it.◆

Chi is seventeen and was born in what is now called Ho Chi Minh City (Saigon) in the former South Vietnam. She came to the United States when she was three. She grew up in the suburbs of Washington, D.C., where her family owns a Vietnamese restaurant and a beauty parlor.

CHI
2 THE YEAR OF THE TIGER

I was the first born of twin sisters. My twin died one or two days later. I was born in 1977. My parents left Vietnam before any of the rest of our family. I escaped in a boat with my grandparents when I was three years old.

We were in the boat for over two weeks. The boat was tight and hot, and very crowded. My grandfather had to hold me on his shoulders, up near the hold, so I could breathe. My grandfather tells me that I was very sick and weak.

At that time, there were a lot of people escaping by boat, and out at sea there were pirates. Some of the pirates would board the boats and rape the women. Some would steal whatever they found, then throw the people into the sea.

Many children were left orphaned or abandoned by the war.

Before I left, we lived in Saigon. That's where my mother's side of the family comes from. My father's side of the family is from Da Nang. After my parents came to the States, I lived with my grandparents in Saigon.

My grandmother died on the way to the United States. She had a heart attack on the boat. They cremated her and put her ashes in a pot. Each year we celebrate the anniversary of her death. Two years after we came here, my grandfather dumped her ashes into the sea. I don't know why he did that, and I wish he hadn't.

My relatives who have visited Vietnam still talk about the house where my grandparents lived.

They say it's haunted. When I was small and we were living there, my uncle would see shadows moving across the room. It was haunted before my grandmother died. And now that she's dead I think it's more haunted. I hear from my cousin that it's all shut down. I have a great curiosity about it. I want to go and see it.

My mom's side of the family are really Americanized. But every once in a while when we get together for family reunions they start to talk about life in Vietnam. They reminisce, and they make me want to go back. They talk about New Year—how the shops were open all day and all night. They remember all the activity, the fun, and the feeling of celebration.

I've heard about the money in Vietnam today. Money goes a long way. You can get a bowl of beef noodle soup for about five cents. Here it costs five dollars. I think there's opportunity in Vietnam now. I want to go back, but I also don't want to.

I don't want to go when I see my cousins who have recently come over from Vietnam. They are really sick. They're rude and greedy. I've heard the people in Vietnam are like that. If you don't give them money they can be nasty. People in Vietnam have the idea that people here have millions of dollars. They have no sense of money. I'm afraid I won't fit in if I go back.

I'm really interested in my culture. I don't want to lose it. I still speak Vietnamese with my friends.

I don't understand Americans who tell me not to speak my native tongue. I am Vietnamese, I tell them. You speak English. I want to speak my language.

I see part-Asians and Asians here who seem to want to be another color. I think, that's your problem! I'm happy with what I am. As a matter of fact, I think they should teach Vietnamese in schools. There are a lot of immigrants here. I think they should teach Vietnamese instead of French.

I live with my mom now and my dad's parents and nephew, my mom's brother, and his daughter. We are nine people in a six-bedroom house.

My grandmother expects a lot of me. She knows I don't love her. If I date someone, she's just nosing into my business. I go home and go to my room. And that's it. I feel like I'm watched over. I have no privacy.

My grandmother doesn't care whether or not I see Vietnamese guys. My parents would prefer that I see Vietnamese guys, but they know I'm not going to. I'm not interested in anybody now. There are a lot of Asians in the school. It's fun to see Vietnamese guys. It's fun to speak to them in Vietnamese and talk about Vietnam. My family owns a beauty parlor, Prestige, in Arlington, Virginia, and a restaurant, the Saigon Inn, in Georgetown in Washington, D.C. I've worked in both

At sixteen, this young girl has lived a perilous life. After fleeing Vietnam in an attempt to reach the United States, she was abducted by pirates in the South China Sea. She is now in a camp for boat people in Thailand waiting to be sent back to Vietnam.

places. Right now I'm doing a lot of community service. I go to homeless shelters and talk to the kids. I'm really involved in it.

My parents want me to work to keep me away from guys. I want to go to college after high school. I want to be an attorney. I want to practice criminal law, perhaps be a prosecutor. And I want to go to Vietnam with my husband on my honeymoon.◆

Duy is sixteen. He came to the United States in 1988 from Ho Chi Minh City. His father was an architect in Vietnam. He now lives with his family in Portland, Oregon.

3
DUY
A BETTER LIFE

I came to the United States from Saigon when I was eleven. I went to school in Saigon, Leloi Grade School. The school had grades one through five and there were about 500 kids. I'd walk to school or ride my bike. We had to wear a uniform—blue pants and white shirt. School was in the morning—from 7:00 to 11:30. You had to stay in one room, and different teachers came. We were taught by both men and women, young and old. It was the same curriculum we have in the United States. There was some political training, but in grade school they didn't teach much politics. I enjoyed sports most in my Vietnamese school. I played soccer—goalie or forward.

At home I lived with my mother and father. I have one older brother and one older sister. In Vietnam, my father was an architect. Here, he works in a restaurant. He's frustrated sometimes because he's not able to be an architect anymore. **29**

The free-market economy in Vietnam has brought opportunities to many. This man works for a company that is a joint venture between South Korean and Japanese businesses operating in Vietnam.

We left as part of the Orderly Departure program. My parents applied for visas and then had to wait a few years. They wanted to leave because the economy wasn't so good and they wanted a better life for us kids.

My parents had suffered in Vietnam. From 1975 to 1978, my father was in a concentration camp as part of the Communist reeducation program. Not only was he a professional person, but he was a lieutenant in the South Vietnamese Army.

What I remember about coming to the United States is leaving by plane from Saigon. It was a big adventure. We lived in a camp in Bangkok for a week. Then we went to Tokyo. We had a short layover and then flew to Seattle, then Portland. We were met by my aunt and uncle. My uncle manages a company. He helped with the money to come here.

My first impression when I came to Portland was how different everything was. The streets weren't as crowded. I spoke a little English when I came, but it was hard to understand people. I went to newcomers' school for about three months to learn English. Then I went into regular school. At first I had a hard time in regular school because of the language. School here is not so hard and not so easy. It's just okay. My goals now are to finish high school and go to college. I haven't made up my mind what I want to study.◆

Van came to the United States in 1990 from Ho Chi Minh City. She settled with her family in Portland, Oregon. An outstanding student and a devout Catholic, Van plans to go to college to study biochemistry and medicine.

VAN
A PICTURE OF HO CHI MINH

I came to the United States when I was 13. My family lived in Saigon near the biggest airport. My father worked with a company that sold cameras. My mother stayed home because in Vietnam most women don't work. Both my mother's and father's families came from the middle of Vietnam, from Hue. They came to Saigon when they were about three years old. Both family sides became Catholic long, long ago.

I went to public school in Saigon, and I went to church on Sunday and studied the Bible. Our house in Saigon was a good house, but on a rainy day it was flooded. I really liked it . . . I like to play in water . . . no, I'm just kidding! I lived with my brother and sister. I'm the oldest. We lived with my grandparents, aunts and uncles, too. The whole big family lived together. It wasn't crowded. We liked to live that way, you know.

Ho Chi Minh was instrumental in bringing communism to Vietnam.

We went to school from 7:30 to 12:00 in the morning. Not a long day like here. In elementary school we were off Thursdays and Sundays, but in middle school we went six days a week. The curriculum was much harder than here. There were no multiple-choice tests; we had to write out the whole answer. It was a very good way to learn. When I came here it was easy for me because of my studies in Vietnam.

We didn't have any political training, but Ho Chi Minh's picture was in every classroom. They (the Communists) said he was a good guy. They said our country was very rich when it was really very poor. I hate them. Our government was made up of people who weren't even educated. Many of them just fought in the war and then got into power. They made us believe in stuff we don't believe. And they hated the Catholics.

My parents decided to come here to give us a better future. They didn't think about their own future. In my country you could never buy a house or car. Here we can.

When we came to the United States, my aunt and uncle sponsored us. They had worked for the government in Vietnam, and so in 1975 they had to get out. They paid for our airline tickets, and they helped us when we first came. My parents started to work 18 days after we arrived. First, my father and my mother worked in different hotels; now they both work in the same hotel.

When I first came, I didn't speak English. I didn't understand anything! When I first went to school it was awful. I didn't know which room to go to. In my country people stay in the same room. Other Vietnamese in the school helped me.

The school put me into classes that were too easy for me. I found a Vietnamese teacher, and he helped me. I was soon able to move to a more advanced level of math. By the beginning of my sophomore year I was an A student. I worked very hard. When I got home I just studied, studied, studied. I made no entertainment for myself. Now I allow myself one hour of entertainment. Just one hour!

I had trouble in physical education. The Americans are bigger and stronger. They run faster. But I pray a lot. I believe God will give me the grade I want in PE. I pray to Mary, the mother of God. I love her. I love her more than everything. She made a big change in my life. It's very personal. Something happened in 1988. Since then, I can feel her and talk to her every day. She is the mother of Jesus.

I miss Vietnam. I cried almost every day when I first came here. I missed my grandmother, aunt, and uncle, all the people on my mother's side. I plan to go and visit Vietnam when I graduate from high school.

I'm going to take my SAT in May. I'm interested in biochemistry. When I go to graduate school I'll continue in biochemistry. But I'm also interested in medicine. I haven't decided which way I'll go.

Seafood is a staple of the Vietnamese diet. Here women sort and sell squid and shrimp just unloaded from a fishing boat.

Next year, I'm going to go to Reed College, Lewis and Clark College, or Portland State University. I've already been accepted into all three programs. Reed and Lewis and Clark gave me full scholarships.

I don't compare myself with other people. I only try and do my best. And I pray to God.◆

Hanh, fifteen, comes from the southernmost rice-growing region in Vietnam. His father was a farmer. Hanh and his family left Vietnam in 1992. They now live in Jacksonville, Florida. Hanh plans to go to college to study mathematics. He wants to join the United States Navy.

HANH
ALL THE WAY SOUTH

I come from Tra Vinh in South Vietnam, all the way in the south, a rice-growing region. I was 13 when I left Vietnam. My whole family left. We had a sponsor in the United States. In Vietnam, my father was a farmer; he grew rice and bananas. My mother helped my father in the fields, and she helped him sell the rice.

The school I went to in Vietnam was different than American schools. They teach all subjects in one classroom. They had a lot of dictation and math. It was very hard, but not harder than American schools.

Our house in Vietnam was small, not like an American house. The roof was made out of a tree, a Cay Dau tree. The floor was earth.

When I was 12 years old I played at being a cowboy. When I had the money I played billiards. **39**

American troops were sent to Vietnam in an attempt to protect southern Vietnam from communism, which had been instituted in northern Vietnam.

When I didn't have any money, I played soccer and volleyball. I would like to go back to Vietnam, perhaps after college.

I'm the oldest child, and I have three younger sisters. My family is Buddhist. In the U.S. I go to church every Sunday, but in Vietnam I practiced Buddhism. My family goes to church, except my father; he works all day Sunday cooking in a Chinese restaurant.

I came by plane from Saigon. It was the first time I had been in an airplane. We flew to the Philippines, where we studied English for six months. We had an American supervisor. Then we flew to Korea, to California for fifteen or twenty minutes, to New Mexico, changed planes again, and then to Florida. We flew for a day and a night.

There are many new foods here in America. My favorite is chicken pot pie.

The people here are different. They're white and they're black, but we are brown. In the school where I go there are a lot of Vietnamese students. People are nice to me. I get along well with my teachers. In Vietnam, if we didn't do our homework or broke the rules, we were slapped on the hand. They don't do that here.

My family came to the United States because they wanted to have freedom. They wanted to make a lot of money to help our poor relatives in Vietnam. My mom works long hours in a Laundromat. She sends money to Vietnam.

During the war, my father fought in the South Vietnamese Army. I heard from him that the Americans came to help us. After the war, he married my mom and became a farmer. He is now thirty-eight. He didn't have to go to a concentration camp after the war. My grandfather is dead; the North Vietnamese shot him during the war.

I plan to go to college. I'd like to study math and English. I'd like to go into the Navy. I did the Navy program for young people last year. I want to get involved with aircraft. I want to fly. I want to serve in the American military.◆

Nica, nineteen, is half Cambodian and half Vietnamese. She was born in 1975 when Vietnam and Cambodia were at war. Her father was a member of the army in South Vietnam. She left Cambodia and crossed the border into Thailand in 1981 with her family. She now lives in the Bronx in New York City. She plans to study pre-med in college.

6

NICA
IMPRISONED BY THE VC

My mom is Cambodian, but my father is Vietnamese. We practice Vietnamese customs in my house. For example, we celebrate Vietnamese New Year more than Cambodian. We eat Vietnamese delicacies. We sit around and sing like Vietnamese. Cambodians go to parties. Vietnamese celebrate the New Year with a tree; we put red envelopes containing money on its branches like blossoms.

When I was born in 1975, the war was going on between Vietnam and Cambodia. My father was a soldier in the South Vietnamese Army. From about 1975 to 1980 he was imprisoned by the Viet Cong. He doesn't talk about it much. And neither does my mother.

I don't know how they met. I don't know much about their past. They're very secretive. I'm not sure why. Maybe because Vietnam was a bad

Escaping from a country is a traumatic experience, especially when facing the threat of being returned to that country, as do these people in a camp in Hong Kong.

experience for them. When they talk about it, I personally see a lot of death. And, you know, I don't know why anyone would want to talk about that. My father's family were murdered by Communists. Who wants to think about that?

When they talk about their past, they talk about funny things, incidents from their childhood. It was hard for them to be together, to be married. It wasn't just the language barrier, but also because of the fact that Vietnamese and Cambodians don't like each other. When they fight, my mom calls my dad VC (Viet Cong).

I remember one episode when we were escaping from Cambodia. We were going through barbed wire that was tearing at our clothing, but we could not make a sound or the VC would capture us. All we could hear were the crickets. This was in 1981. All I remember is Mom carrying me. We left at night. We heard soldiers talking. We walked for hours, over the border into Thailand.

I remember it was hot in Thailand. We only stayed a few days. Then we went on a boat to the United States. Mom tells me that the boat was crowded. A lot of people were sick. My step-mother's husband died on the boat. His body was thrown overboard. From then on, she never ate fish, because she saw the fish eating the dead bodies in the sea.

My first memory of the United States was the little peanuts on the airplane. I also remember the cities at night. They were lit up and looked so nice, not like in the daytime when they look dirty. They looked tranquil and serene. In the daytime it looks as if no one cares. We were able to come to the United States because we were sponsored by an aunt and uncle on my father's side, who lived in Brooklyn.

When we came here, I spoke a little bit of English. I learned it from my father, who learned it in prison. I was accepted more by the Cambodians than the Vietnamese. Cambodians are more gossipy and more easy-going than Vietnamese. Cambodians tend to care about the appearance of a person.

Life for children was difficult at best in Vietnam during and after the war. They arrived in Hong Kong in boatloads.

Vietnamese care about appearances too, but not that much. Since I'm so used to both peoples, I don't see much difference between them. I used to see differences in their faces, in color, in the way they talked. But I don't so much anymore.

When I graduate from high school, I want to go to college and study pre-med. I'd like to go back to Cambodia or Vietnam. I saw so much suffering there. You see little kids dying of fever and mumps. The clinics are not clean. There's not many doctors. All the best doctors are in the United States. Who wants to go to a country where they won't pay you well? But I want to go back even though I wouldn't get paid that well. Eventually I would come back to the U.S.

It doesn't really matter to me whom I marry, whether he's Vietnamese or Cambodian or American. I always seem to end up with Vietnamese guys, however. When my mom remarried, she married an American of Arab descent, a Palestinian. I live with my father and my stepmom, who is Vietnamese. I have a younger sister who was born here.

I want to say one more thing. I think Vietnam is progressing really well. Their economy is booming. They may not be a Third World nation for much longer. They always make sure you know they exist. People from Australia know about Vietnamese music. They can sing Vietnamese songs. They know the words. How many people that aren't Chinese can sing Chinese songs?◆

Ha, eighteen, comes from a small farming village east of Ho Chi Minh City. Her father was an American soldier who fought in the Vietnam War; she has never met him. She now lives in Dallas, Texas, goes to school, studies English, and works as a dietician. She would like to go to college.

7
HA
RICE FOR BREAKFAST

I have been in the United States one year. I lived in a small village in Vietnam called Thach Ha. It's in the south, east of Saigon. The village had about three thousand people. I lived there with my mother and my sister and my brother. I'm the youngest child. I don't know who my father is.

My mother was a farmer. She grew beans and tomatoes and pineapples. She sold them in the market town, a village near Saigon.

In Vietnam, I went to school until eighth grade. And then I had to help my mother and my sister on the farm. I was fifteen years old when I started working on the farm. We woke up at about five o'clock. We ate rice for breakfast. You know in Vietnam we always eat rice. After breakfast we went to the farm and helped my mother plant and pick the vegetables and go to the market.

Two Vietnamese vendors with baskets full of fresh seafood.

We worked very hard. Sometimes we'd get home at six o'clock, sometimes at seven. Then we'd eat dinner. Rice, rice, rice. Every day the same. Rice and fish and vegetables. After dinner, sometimes we visited my relatives. I don't have a grandmother or grandfather. I have an uncle, who lived alone. I had a friend named Trang. We did things together. I'd tell her about myself and she'd tell me about herself. I was very sad when I came to the United States and had to leave her.

We came to the U.S. because a long time ago Americans came to Vietnam, and my mom made friends with one of them. This was during the war. After the war, he went back to the United States, but I don't know his name or where he's living. That's how my mother had the kids in our family. We came here because some Vietnamese people told my mom there was a way for people with American fathers to go to the U.S.

When we left, we took an airplane from Saigon. It was fun, but I was scared! From Vietnam I went to the Philippines for seven months. I lived in a camp where I studied English. I took another airplane from the Philippines to the United States. First I went to California and then to Texas.

I was very happy for me and my family. My brother got work in a restaurant, and my sister's a seamstress. My mother stays at home, and I go to school. I like school. My teacher is very good, and I have a good friend. I study math and science. I

A view of Ho Chi Minh City, formerly Saigon, in 1976, shortly after the reunification of Vietnam.

also practice speaking and reading English—and acting, too. I would like to be an actress.

After school, I have a job cooking dietary food. I work only weekends. I think I want to go to college, if I can get the money. I'd like to become an accountant, but I don't know. I think it's very difficult to do.◆

Lien, seventeen, lived in Ho Chi Minh City until she was five years old. Then she moved to Cambodia. She left Cambodia when she was seven and escaped across the border into Thailand. In Thailand, she lived in a refugee camp for about six months. Since coming to the United States she has lived in Philadelphia and San Francisco. She is currently living in the Bronx, finishing high school.

LIEN
A WAR FOR POWER

I lived in Saigon until I was five years old. Then we moved to Cambodia. I moved there with my mother, four brothers, and three sisters. My dad was already in Cambodia. It was easier at that time to make a living in Cambodia. In Saigon, the Communists forced my two brothers to work for them, but my brothers kept escaping. Then they forced my mother to work for them. That's why we moved.

I remember we lived in a place like a farm, but my house was in front of a graveyard. A Vietnamese cemetery is not like an American cemetery. Every grave has dirt on top of it like a little hill. My house was kind of crowded. Half of the house was a raised sleeping area where we all slept in a row. It was covered with a curtain. The other part of the house was a living-cooking-eating area.

Volunteers load a rowboat with fireworks in preparation for celebrating national Independence Day in Vietnam.

I don't remember where we lived in Cambodia, what town. My father was working, sewing things. We made toys from paper, like paper snakes, that we sold. We lived in an apartment there. I remember we lived on the third floor. Cambodia seemed different from Vietnam because on the street they had lots of markets selling food and vegetables.

I left Cambodia when I was about seven years old. One night my brothers fixed everything up. They had food and stuff, and they said we were going to my grandmother's, but then we walked into the woods with two guides and a priest. We walked three nights through the jungle, and we heard gunshots. We slept on the ground in the daytime. We had to lie on the ground all day.

We finally got to Thailand. At first they put us in jail. They took all our jewelry and money. We were in the jail for a week or two. They took me out by myself because they thought I was cute. Then we went to the camps.

We were in the camps for about six months. It was kind of scary because a war was going on around us. Guns shooting every night. We were always packing our stuff in case we had to leave. Six months later they announced that we were going to go to a different place in Thailand. I don't know who was taking us to these different places.

We arrived at a place where they took our pictures, gave us IDs, and put us on an airplane. We flew to the United States, to New York City.

Since coming to the United States I've lived in many places. At first no one would sponsor us. We moved from New York to Chester, Pennsylvania, where a Catholic priest sponsored us. I stayed with an Italian woman there. She bought me clothes and took care of me for a while.

I went to California for a while because my brothers thought they could make a better living in San Francisco. We stayed there a year and a half. While we were in California, we had a letter from my father saying my mother was dead. My brother read the letter out loud and we were all crying. My father is still living but I don't know where he is.

It turned out my brothers had trouble making a living in California, so we moved back to Chester. We moved to Philadelphia, and then to Massachusetts. My brother made me stay with our aunt. I don't know why. I can't live with my aunt. She's too difficult. She's old-fashioned. She says girls have to stay in the house. I couldn't do anything about it.

When I was 14 I moved back to Philadelphia and stayed with my brother, who was working at a factory. My other brother got married and came to Philadelphia, and I moved in with them. During all this time, I tried to go to school. I missed some grades. I think I have a lot of time left to go in school, but I have a lot of life experience. Sometimes I feel lonely, like I've had a tough life and I have no one to talk to.

Then the brother I was living with broke up with his wife. He moved to Texas and I stayed with her. Then she started drinking and gambling a lot. She would leave her kids with me, sometimes overnight, and I'd miss school. I got tired of this, and I got on a bus. I don't know what I was thinking or where I was going. I just thought I'd take a bus to New York City.

In New York I didn't know anybody. I just came. That was on March 23, 1994. When I got off the bus, I waited until nighttime. Then I started to get scared and I asked the police where to go and they told me to go to Covenant House. At Covenant House they suggested I go to St. Rita's (a

Tourism in Vietnam has blossomed in recent years. A boat sails amidst the 3,000 islands of HaLong Bay in Vietnam, the future site of a major resort area.

refugee organization) in the Bronx, and St. Rita's found me a family to stay with.

Every place I go people have been nice to me. I want to go back to school, find a part-time job, and stay here in New York, hopefully in one place. I have to sleep in the living room of the place I'm staying now, so I may have to move. I don't know. We'll have to see.◆

Glossary

ancestor worship Religion based on reverence of dead ancestors.

Buddhism Religion and philosophic system popular in central and eastern Asia.

Caodaism Religion originating in Vietnam whose practitioners commune with the dead through a medium.

colonialism System by which a country maintains foreign colonies in order to exploit them economically.

Confucianism The teachings of Confucius introduced into the Chinese religion.

domination Rule or control by superior power or influence.

famine An acute and general shortage of food.

guerrilla Member of a small force of irregular soldiers making surprise raids.

immigration Coming into a new country in order to settle there.

Islam Religion in which the supreme deity is Allah and the chief prophet is Muhammad.

refugee Person who flees from home or country to seek safety elsewhere.

Taoism A Chinese religion and philosophy based on the doctrines of Lao-tzu.

Viet Cong The North Vietnamese military force. 61

For Further Reading

Brown, Gene. *The Nation in Turmoil: Civil Rights and the Vietnam War.* New York: Twenty-First Century Books, Inc., 1993.

Downs, Frederick, Jr. *No Longer Enemies, Not Yet Friends: An American Soldier Returns to Vietnam.* New York: Pocket Books, 1993.

Griffiths, John. *The Last Day in Saigon.* North Pomfret, VT: Trafalgar Square, 1987.

Hanh, Thich N. *A Taste of Earth and Other Legends of Vietnam.* Berkeley: Parallax Press, 1993.

Hauptly, Denis J. *In Vietnam.* New York: Macmillan Children's Book Group, 1985.

Hoobler, Dorothy, and Hoobler, Thomas. *Vietnam: An Illustrated History.* New York: Alfred A. Knopf Books for Young Readers, 1990.

Nhuong, Nuynh Quang. *The Land I Lost: Adventures of a Boy in Vietnam.* New York: HarperCollins Children's Books, 1990.

Terry, Wallace. *Bloods: An Oral History of the Vietnam War by Black Veterans.* New York: Ballantine Books, Inc., 1985.

Index

ABOUT THE AUTHOR

Kenneth Wapner is a freelance writer. He is the author of *Catskill Rambles*, a book of narrative essays about growing up. He lives in Woodstock, New York, with his son, Elijah.

PHOTO CREDITS

pp. 22, 28, 42 © Erica Degen; p. 38 © Valerie Tekavec; all other photos © AP/Wide World Photos

LAYOUT AND DESIGN

Kim Sonsky